What Jesus did

**Bible Stories retold by
Jean and Jennifer Rees
and Mary Batchelor**

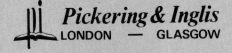
Pickering & Inglis
LONDON — GLASGOW

ISBN 0 7208 2265 3
Cat. No. 11/4202

Printed in Great Britain

The Great Storm

It was evening on the crowded beach at Capernaum. Jesus was standing in a boat which was just a little way off from the shore. All day long He had been speaking to the people, and they had been happy to sit hour after hour listening to all He had to say.

Peter and Andrew were getting anxious. "He has not had one minute's rest for days now," said Peter.

"No," replied Andrew, "and He hasn't had time to eat either."

The other disciples also were concerned about their Master, so it was with a sigh of relief that they heard Jesus finish speaking to the crowds, and turn to them and say, "Let us sail across the lake to the other side."

The disciples didn't need to be told twice. Telling the crowd to go home, they quickly got the boat ready for sailing, and when they were all on board, they turned the boat round. Slowly it began to move away from the shore.

As darkness came down, the disciples were excited at the thought of a few days' holiday away from the crowds. They knew their Master needed a rest, and they were going to make sure that He got it.

At the back of the boat was a cushion on which the person who steered the boat usually sat. The disciples let Jesus lie with His head on the cushion, and soon He was fast asleep.

The night grew darker, and it was very still. Then, suddenly, everything changed. A crack of lightning lit up the frightened faces of the disciples, and thunder seemed to shout at them from all directions. Then the wind and rain hit them, and whipped the sea up into great waves which swept over the side of the boat.

It was no use trying to row the boat, so, drawing in their oars, the disciples began to bail out the water that had come into the boat. But it all seemed so useless. No sooner had they thrown the water overboard than another wave smashed against the side and more water splashed into the boat.

The little boat began to creak and groan. "We're sinking!" shouted Andrew, "I've never seen such a storm."

"Where is Jesus?" cried one of the other disciples. Turning round, the disciples were amazed to see Him peacefully asleep, His head still resting on the cushion.

Making his way to the back of the boat, Peter shook Jesus until He opened His eyes. "Master," he shouted above the noise of the wind and the waves, "we are sinking. Are you not worried? Do you not care?"

Very calmly, Jesus stood up. He looked up to the grey sky, and then out on to the raging water. "Peace, be still!" He shouted.

And there was peace. As the terrified disciples watched, the wind dropped to a gentle breeze, the great waves became ripples, and the boat rested peacefully in the water.

They continued their journey to the other side of the lake. The disciples did not know what to say. Peter whispered to his brother, "You know, Andrew, I was frightened in the storm, but I was even more frightened when I saw the wind and the waves do just as Jesus told them."

Mark 4:1,35-41

The Boy and his Picnic

The boy lived in a village by the Sea of Galilee. One evening, as he lay in bed, he was listening to the men talking in the road outside his house. On hearing Jesus' name being mentioned, he sat up and strained his ears to listen.

"Yes," one man was saying, "Jesus is at that place along the coast, where the grass grows. He's speaking to thousands of people and has been there for two whole days."

I must go there tomorrow, thought the boy. If I don't, I may never have a better chance of seeing Him.

Early next morning he set off, carrying the little picnic lunch of five barley loaves and two small fish which his mother had packed for him. It was a long walk to where Jesus was, and when the boy reached the place he saw a great crowd of people. He had never seen so many people before.

When Jesus began to speak, everyone became very still. All day long they listened to the wonderful things Jesus was saying.

When evening came, some of the people became restless. "Some of us have had nothing to eat for three days," explained one man, "so we are very hungry."

Then the boy thought, I wonder if Jesus has had anything to eat? Holding his picnic lunch tight in his hand, he began to make his way towards Jesus. One of Jesus' disciples, Andrew, saw him and with a kind look and a smile asked, "You look worried. Can I help you?"

"Oh, please," said the boy, "I thought Jesus might like my lunch."

"I think He might," replied Andrew. "Come and we'll give it to Him."

As they walked towards Jesus, they heard Him say, "We cannot send all these people away before we have given them something to eat."

"But Master," replied Philip, another of Jesus' disciples, "we have no food to give them."

It was just then that Andrew arrived. "Master, this boy has five barley loaves and two small fish, but they will not go far among all these people," smiled Andrew.

Jesus took the little bundle from the boy, and very quietly said, "Thank you."

Then everything seemed to happen at once, and they watched in amazement. Jesus told everyone to sit down. Then He prayed to His Father in heaven, thanking Him for the food and asking for His blessing on it.

Jesus then took the first loaf, broke it up and, putting some fish inside, gave the pieces to one of His disciples to give to the hungry people. He continued sharing out the bread and fish to the disciples so that they could take it to the people.

"I thought I had only five loaves," said the boy to himself in wonder as he watched Jesus handing out more and more food for the hungry people to eat.

It seemed hours later that the disciples came to Jesus and said, "Master, everyone has had more than enough. You have fed five thousand people today."

That night when the boy arrived home, he had a marvellous story to tell his mother, of how Jesus had used *his* lunch to feed many, many people.

John 6:2-14

The Man who walked on the Sea

It was the evening of the day that Jesus had fed the five thousand people with the boy's picnic lunch. The crowds had gone away and Jesus was left with His disciples. Calling Peter over to Him, He said, "I must go away alone tonight, Peter, and pray to My Father in heaven. You and the others sail across to the other side of the lake, and I will come to you in the morning."

"But, Peter, how will He find us?" asked Thomas anxiously, as they climbed into the boat. "It will take Him all day to walk round the lake and meet us."

"How should I know what He will do?" replied Peter. "But I do know this; a man who can feed a great crowd with one picnic lunch will surely find His way across the sea to us."

Soon the boat was well out from the shore. "The wind is badly against us tonight," gasped Matthew struggling with his oar. "I hope we are not going to have another storm like the last one."

"This wind is worse than ever," panted Peter. "We've been in the boat for hours and are not making any headway." But his voice was lost in the roar of the gale.

It was then that they saw it.

"Look," said Andrew rather unsteadily. "Before the moon went behind that cloud I was sure I could see something . . . walking . . . on the water."

"Don't be foolish," answered Matthew, "you fishermen are all so fanciful."

"The moon is coming out again," persisted Andrew. "Look, there *is* something there."

"It must be a ghost," screamed James. The figure in the moonlight drew nearer and they clung to one another in terror.

"Look!" shouted Peter at last. "It is the Master."

"It can't be," said Thomas. "Men can't walk on the sea."

"But it *is* the Master," answered Peter, and, stumbling to the side of the boat, he called out, "Lord, if it is You, tell me to come to You on the water."

"Come then," called back the voice they all knew so well.

"Peter," gasped Thomas, "you can't do that. You'll drown."

"Oh, yes I can," said Peter as he jumped out of the boat.

Breathlessly the others in the boat watched as Peter ran towards Jesus. Then Peter made his great mistake. He stopped looking at Jesus and began to wonder how it was that he did not sink. He looked at the great waves all around him, and then back at the boat. Forgetting that Jesus was there, he began to sink. Soon the water was up to his waist, then his shoulders and suddenly it was over his head.

I shall drown, he thought wildly. Thomas was right.

Gasping for breath, he came up once again and shouted with all his might, "Lord, save me."

Down he went again, the waters closing once more over his head. As he struggled up, a firm hand caught him and pulled him out. Peter was so surprised to find himself standing again firmly on his feet that for once he could not speak.

"You don't trust Me much," said Jesus. "Why did you doubt that I would look after you?"

Peter's face was red with shame as he followed Jesus back to the boat.

"I will never stop trusting Him again," he said to himself as he climbed into the boat.

With Jesus in the boat, the wind dropped, and soon they reached the other side of the lake in safety.

Matthew 14:23-32

The King came to Jerusalem

Jesus and His friends set off on the journey to Jerusalem. As they went along the twisting roads, Jesus walked ahead on His own. His heart was heavy because He knew that when He reached the great city He must suffer and die. He and His Father God had planned this long before He came to earth. All people had done so many wrong things that they could never go to be with God in heaven. Yet God loved them so much that He could not bear them to be away from Him for ever.

"Let Me go and die in their place," said

Jesus, "then if they turn to Me and love Me they can come and live with us here in heaven and be our friends."

Now that time had come at last. When Jesus was within a few miles of the city He stopped. Calling two of His disciples towards Him He said, "Do you see that village over there? Go across and as soon as you go into the village street, you will see a donkey tied to a post. Untie it and bring it to Me. If anyone asks you what you are doing, tell them I need it and they will let you have it."

Off went the disciples, and they found it just as Jesus had said. The donkey was standing at the post as the people walked up and down the village street. Untying the rope from the post, they led the donkey out of the village and took it back to Jesus. Then, instead of a saddle, the disciples spread their coats over the donkey's back, for Jesus to sit on. He was ready to go.

As Jesus rode into Jerusalem on that little donkey, He knew all the terrible things that would soon happen to Him. There were crowds on the road, all making their way to Jerusalem, but none of them knew what Jesus was thinking. As He rode towards the city, the crowds began to shout and cheer Jesus. Many of them took off their coats and spread them like a carpet on the road to show that they were making way for someone important. Others ran ahead and cut down branches from nearby trees and spread them on the road.

Then the people began to sing and shout praises to God. They used the words of one of their hymns. "Hosanna to the Son of David! Blessed is He who comes in the name of the Lord!"

Everyone in the city heard the noise, and many came out to see the strange procession. As Jesus rode through the city gate and along the city streets, many stood watching and some began to ask, "Who is this?"

They were soon to get an answer, because the crowds began to shout out, "This is the prophet Jesus from Nazareth in Galilee."

And so all Jerusalem came to know that Jesus had arrived in the city.

Mark 11:1-10

As the disciples walked with Jesus through the city streets of Jerusalem the sun shone brightly down. It would be a relief after walking along the dry, dusty roads to take off their sandals and have their feet fresh and clean.

In many eastern homes there would be a slave ready to wash the feet of any guests arriving at the house. But where there was no slave, there would be a large waterpot filled with water and beside it a basin so that the guests could wash one another's feet.

When Jesus and His disciples arrived at the house where they were going to share a special meal together, they made their way to the upstairs room where everything had been prepared. In the corner of the room was the waterpot and the basin—but there was no slave.

As they had walked along the road the disciples had been arguing among themselves about which of them was the most important of Jesus' disciples. They all wanted to be the most important. So when they arrived at the house, none of the disciples was willing to wash the others' feet, because that would have shown that they were not the most important.

They all sat round the room, proudly looking at one another, watching to see who would be the first to fill the basin with water.

At last someone did get up. It wasn't Peter or John or Thomas. It wasn't any of the disciples. It was Jesus. He poured water into the basin and took a towel. Then He went round the disciples one by one, pouring water over their dusty feet, and rubbing them with the towel to make them fresh and cool.

How ashamed the disciples felt! They had been too proud to do this, but Jesus their Master had been willing to wait on them.

When Jesus came to Simon Peter, Peter asked, "Lord, are you going to wash my feet?"

"Yes, I am," said Jesus. "One day you will understand what I am doing to you."

Peter drew up his feet away from Jesus. " am not good enough. You are never going to wash my feet," he blurted out.

Quietly Jesus spoke to Peter, "Everyone who wants to belong to Me must let Me make him a clean new person all through."

Then Peter gladly took his turn. He knew he needed a clean heart as well as clean feet and only Jesus could give it to him.

When Jesus had washed the feet of all the twelve disciples, He put down the basin and sat down.

By this time the disciples were too ashamed to say anything. They sheepishly looked at one another.

Then Jesus spoke. "Do you understand what I have done for you?" He asked. "You call me your Master and Lord—and I am. Yet I have washed your feet. You also should care for one another. The one who is willing to look after the needs of others is the one who in God's eyes is truly great and truly happy."

John 13:4-1

Jesus the King

The Jewish leaders held a special meeting. "We must get rid of Jesus," they all agreed. Instead of loving Jesus for all the good things He did and said, they hated Him because so many people followed Him and because He gave them a guilty conscience. They wondered where they could find Jesus on His own and take Him prisoner. They were delighted when Judas Iscariot, one of Jesus' own disciples, offered to tell them where He would be, away from the crowds.

The plan worked. They crept into the garden where Jesus was praying one evening and seized Him. "Tomorrow we will go to the Roman ruler and persuade him to put Jesus to death."

Early next morning they took Jesus to Pilate, the Roman ruler. Pilate did not like these troublesome Jewish leaders. He asked them roughly:

"What has this man done wrong?"

"He makes Himself a nuisance," they replied. "He teaches the people wrong things and He says He is a king."

Pilate went across to Jesus, "Are you really a king?" he asked.

"I am not the kind of king you imagine," Jesus answered. "My followers are not soldiers who will fight battles to save me. I have not been born to conquer countries but to tell everyone the truth about God."

Pilate was puzzled but he was sure Jesus had done nothing wrong. He knew the Jews wanted to kill Him because they were jealous and spiteful.

"I have talked to the prisoner," Pilate told the Jews. "He has not done any of the bad things

throng the narrow Jerusalem streets. Pilate usually set free a prisoner on this special festival which was called Passover, so now he had a new idea for letting Jesus go.

"Shall I set king Jesus free this Passover time?" he asked the crowd below. But the Jewish leaders had told the crowds what to shout. They all answered "No—we want Barabbas". Barabbas was a Jew who had been sentenced for murder. Soon the crowds joined in the chant "Nail Jesus to the cross! Nail Jesus to the cross!"

Jesus stood quite still and calm as Pilate paced anxiously up and down and the crowds jostled and shouted below. He knew that He would die, not because these wicked men were too strong but because He wanted to give His life for the sins of the world.

At last Pilate could not stand the noise and threats any longer.

"Take him," he shouted to the Jewish leaders and ordered his soldiers to lead Jesus away. They would fasten Him by nails through His hands and feet to a high wooden beam until He died. Jesus began the journey to the cross outside the city and His sad disciples followed far behind.

Luke 22:47;23:1-24

you say. He does not deserve to die." But the Jews shouted at the tops of their voices, "Kill Him. Kill Him!"

By this time a big crowd had collected and Pilate was frightened they would start trouble. Everyone was excited because there was a special Jewish celebration that day—there were processions and feasts and many visitors

A Breakfast by the Lake

It was a lovely evening with the waves of the Sea of Galilee gently rippling along the shore. Seven men were sitting by the water's edge talking to one another. They were the disciples of Jesus. They all knew now that their Master was alive again and they were so glad. How often they spoke to each other of all that had happened and of the times He had suddenly visited them since His resurrection.

Suddenly Peter the fisherman jumped up. "I'm going fishing," he said, and he began to make his way towards the boat.

"We'll come with you," shouted the others as they got to their feet. Some of them fetched the nets, while the others began to pull the boat down to the water's edge. When everything was ready they pushed the boat into the water.

As they rowed away from the shore, darkness came down and they settled to a night's fishing. They let the net down into the sea, and after a time drew it in again.

"Not a single fish," said Thomas, looking at the empty net, "I wonder where they have gone. Let's try again."

So the net was put into the water once more. Drawing it in a second time, they saw it was still empty. So it went on all night. As dawn began to break and the sun began to rise over the eastern shore, they had to admit that they hadn't caught a single fish.

They drew near to the shore, and through the early morning haze they saw someone standing on the beach.

He called to them across the waves, "Friends, have you caught anything?"

"No, nothing at all," they shouted back.

"Do as I tell you," the stranger called back to them, "cast your net on the other side of the boat, and you'll catch some fish."

The disciples looked at one another. "If we couldn't catch any fish during the night, we're not likely to get any now that it's daylight," said one of them. "Anyway, there's no harm in trying."

The disciples did as the stranger had said. Suddenly they felt a strain on the net. They began to pull the net back on board the boat. To their great surprise, the net was full of fish. In fact, there were so many fish that they couldn't haul the net back into the boat.

One of the disciples thought this very strange. He raised his eyes towards the water's edge and took a long look at the stranger still standing on the shore. Suddenly he turned round to Peter and exclaimed: "It is the Lord!"

As soon as Peter heard that, he left the other six to look after the fish and jumping overboard, waded ashore to where Jesus was standing. The others soon followed bringing the boat safely to land, and dragging with them the net full of fish. When they counted, they found they had caught one hundred and fifty-three fish.

Jesus had lighted a little fire on the shore. He knew the disciples would be hungry after their night's work, so He began to make breakfast for them. What a delicious smell! He cooked some of the fish which they had caught and made some bread. When it was all ready, Jesus and His seven disciples sat around on the shore and ate together the meal He had prepared. How glad the disciples were to be with Jesus again!

John 21:2-13